WHAT JACK
TAUGHT GRANDPA

T5-CCX-263

WHAT JACK TAUGHT GRANDPA

Practical Wisdom from a Knee-High Perspective

Bob Heckman and Sandy Heckman

BROWN BOOKS
PUBLISHING GROUP

WHAT JACK TAUGHT GRANDPA
Practical Wisdom from a Knee-High Perspective

© 2010 by Bob Heckman and Sandy Heckman

All rights reserved. No part of this publication may be reproduced,
stored in any retrieval system, or transmitted in any form or by any means,
mechanical, photocopying, recording, or otherwise, without permission
in writing from the publisher, except by a reviewer,
who may quote brief passages in a review.

Manufactured in the United States of America.

For information, please contact:

Brown Books Publishing Group
16200 North Dallas Parkway, Suite 170
Dallas, Texas 75248

www.brownbooks.com
972-381-0009
A New Era in Publishing™

ISBN-13: 978-1-934812-46-4
ISBN-10: 1-934812-46-3
LCCN: 2009934969
1 2 3 4 5 6 7 8 9 10

To our grandkids—Jack, Ally, Tommy, and Bobby—
and to all grandkids everywhere.

Relive the fun of life through your grandchildren . . .
then hand them back to their parents
when you want to go home!

BEST BUDDIES

"Gotcha, Poppa." Jack giggled as I rubbed the spot where the ball hit me in the chest after it had bounced off the ground. *Bad hop*, I thought to myself. I reached down to retrieve the ball. I tossed it, underhanded, back to him. Jack stretched out his arms and held them steady as he closed his eyes and waited for the ball. It hit his hands and rolled a few feet away. He ran after it, picked it up, and returned to his spot in the shade. He wound up again and launched another throw my way.

"Good catch, Poppa!"

"Great throw, Jack!"

We continued our game of catch for a while before Grammy and I gathered our things to load into the car. As we said our good-byes, Jack caught me at the door and motioned for me to bend down. He had a secret to share.

"Poppa, we'll always be best buddies!"

Scooping him up in a hug, I couldn't speak. But my heart agreed. Yes, Jack, we will always be best buddies.

Life Lesson

Our picnic with Jack's parents, Kathy and Dave, and siblings, Ally and Tommy, was one of many when Jack left me thinking about things he'd said to me. "Best buddies." We've said those words to each other many times since that day at the park. Jack taught me how important it is to say words to others that communicate how special they are to us. Sometimes just a touch on the shoulder or a smile across the dinner table says it all. Sometimes we need to learn from Jack and just say it out loud.

THIS IS FOR YOU

Jack, Ally, Tommy, Grammy, and I clutched our bags of treats and passed around a bucket of popcorn as we waited for the movie to begin. The theater lights dimmed, and Jack's eyes were glued to the screen throughout the previews. As the movie began, Jack dug around in his theater-sized bag of M&M's looking for his favorite color.

A few minutes later, Grammy felt a tap on her arm. Jack beamed in the glow of the movie and held out his hand with his offering—one blue M&M.

"Here, Grammy, this is for you!"

"Thanks, Jack, that's very thoughtful." Grammy smiled and looked at the sole M&M in the palm of her hand.

Something clicked in Jack's mind as he, too, looked at the M&M. It was lonely, even though it was a treasured, blue one.

"Here's more for you, Grammy!" Jack dropped a handful of M&M's in her hand and nodded his head. He knew he'd done something good.

Life Lesson

Jack's parents had always taught him to share. In school, teachers often ask children if they've brought enough treats for everyone. From a young age, we all learn that sharing—toys, food, and chores—is a good thing.

At the movie theater that day, Jack put into practice the principle of sharing. Okay, one blue M&M isn't exactly a handful, but he demonstrated that he understood the importance of sharing his things with others. Jack reminded us that day that the thought behind the actions makes the difference. No matter how small the gift may be, the thought behind sharing is what counts.

Please Take My Order!

The waiter led us to our table, and we settled into our seats. Jack's family was vacationing with us, and one evening we went to a nice restaurant for dinner. It was a quaint place with dim lights and low music, the kind of place where you usually don't take kids. As the adults studied their menus and discussed options with the waiter and each other, Jack watched. After the waiter returned with our drinks, we began ordering. Jack didn't want to be left out. He stood in his chair and raised his hand politely.

"Do you think you might have a little steak out there in the kitchen—and maybe some pasta, too?" The waiter smiled and wrote Jack's order on his pad.

Life Lesson

Jack didn't want to miss his chance. He made sure he was included in the ordering process. Although his mother would've ordered for him, he wanted to be heard. He ordered politely, and when all of us laughed, including the waiter, Jack was confident that a plate of steak and pasta would soon be sitting in front of him.

Jack reminded us that kids want to be a part of the team. They want us to ask them, "What do you think?" or "What would you like?" Too often as adults, we assume we know what's best without considering our children's thoughts and preferences. We move the salt, pepper, and sugar as far away from the children as we can and forget to include them in making decisions.

Even at young ages, kids have a lot to offer, and we need to give them a chance to contribute. Asking a simple question like "What do you like?" or "What do you think?" lets them know they are important, too. And we might just make a "best buddy" in the process!

Move to the Other Side

The covered wagon lumbered along the trail. Jack and his younger sister, Ally, were sitting next to Grammy and me. Dressed in boots and cowboy hats, the kids played the part of frontiersmen—complete with six-guns for protection. This vacation in the mountains included our Western experience with cowboys, horses, and Indians. The kids were chattering about the sights along the trail as we made our way to the bonfire and barbeque dinner. Suddenly, two riders dressed as Indians on the warpath, complete with bows and arrows, war paint, and yelps and screams came riding up alongside our wagon. Jack took one look and scrambled quickly to the other side of the wagon.

"Bye, Poppa! I'm going to sit on the other side for a while!"

Life Lesson

Even with his official cowboy duds and pistols, when confronted with a scary situation, it made more sense for Jack to muster the courage to move. So he did. Sometimes it makes sense to get out of an unfamiliar or even dangerous situation. While this was orchestrated entertainment for the wagon trail ride, many situations we encounter in life aren't all fun and games. Some are downright scary. Some demand that we take a stand and handle the problem. Others may require us to make the decision to leave.

Those are the times we should muster the courage to say "enough." Those are the times we should move to the other side of the wagon.

BEST-SPECIAL-ALL-TIME TREAT

The family was gathered around the dinner table. Finishing his dinner was a supreme effort for Jack that night. After moving the food around on his plate as long as his patience would allow, Jack finally put his fork down and sighed.

"Grammy, if I make my dinner all gone, can I have my best-special-all-time treat?"

Jack didn't ask simply for dessert; he wanted a best-special-all-time-treat. And that could be anything, from fruit to ice cream or maybe a Popsicle. One day we came up with the name, and it stuck. Knighting dessert with an important name made his overwhelming task—eating dinner—seem less daunting. Jack wanted the best-special-all-time treat. The prize was worth the effort.

Life Lesson

Jack reminded us that sometimes, those jobs that loom over us can seem less intimidating when we can look forward to a reward at the end of our efforts. It's about reframing our perspective and looking through fresh eyes. Jack taught me that ordinary things may have the value hidden beyond what we see on the surface. Sometimes things aren't as they appear at first—they might be even better. A cookie is not always a cookie—sometimes it's a best-special-all-time treat.

Enjoy the Moment

Sluuuuurrrrp! Jack drained the last bit of Slurpee through his straw. Jack and I kept our nearest convenience store in business during the summer he was five. He loved riding in our bright red convertible, especially at night. During one evening ride with the top down, he leaned his head back and gazed at the sky.

"Poppa, there aren't any stars tonight."

"You're right, Jack. It's cloudy, so we can't see them."

"Do you like those stars, Poppa?"

"Yes, I do, Jack. Yes, I do."

"Me too, Poppa, me too."

The convertible rides weren't about going some place, they were about spending time together. Talking and enjoying the moment—bonding. Jack understood, and he often expressed his desire for those special times in unusual ways. One evening, as we climbed in the car on a Slurpee outing, Jack informed me of his desire for serious bonding time.

"Poppa, when we drive back home, can we take the longcut instead of the shortcut?"

Life Lesson

Jack's words emphasized the importance of spending quality time together, talking and bonding. Taking our time to hear about each other's friends and sharing stories about the day's activities are good ways of getting to know the hearts of those we love.

Convertible rides with Jack taught this grandpa to forget about arrivals and destinations, to slow down and enjoy the moment. It's OK to take the "longcut." In fact, sometimes, it's a great idea!

I'll Take This End!

The sign at the Florida restaurant read "Come and See the Alligators!" Jack took one look at the sign and made his decision—this was the spot where we would have lunch.

After we were seated, one of the staff approached us, holding an alligator. It was about two feet long. We jumped back when the man extended the critter toward us, asking if we wanted to hold it for a picture. When Jack looked closely, he saw that the alligator's mouth had been gently taped to keep him from biting anything. Jack understood at once.

"I can hold that end," he volunteered.

Jack felt OK about taking the risky end of the creature because he had looked closely and observed an important detail—the alligator's large and sharp teeth wouldn't be a problem. Jack quickly figured out that everything was safe and that he was safe . . . and brave.

Life Lesson

We can learn from Jack. In a new or unfamiliar situation, we can observe details and gather information. We can check out the circumstances and consider options. We may understand that things aren't always as they first appear—some situations require us to investigate a little further. Armed with good information, we can make informed decisions and sound choices.

Our picture of Jack holding the alligator is one of our favorites—the size of Jack's smile is only exceeded by the length of the alligator! The photo brings back memories of that day at the beach when Jack figured out that things aren't always as they may first appear.

KEEP A SENSE OF HUMOR

The well-constructed fort under the dining room table hid an arsenal of Jack's pirate treasures: binoculars, a Happy Meal periscope, a plastic sword, and a trick rope to tie up any unwanted visitors. Today he was a pirate hiding from the admiral of the fleet, and I was his first mate. I looked inside the fort and saw Jack adjusting his eye patch.

"Let's go get some lunch, Jack." My knees were relieved when Jack grabbed his binoculars and emerged from hiding with a shout. "Aye, aye, mate!"

"Grammy asked us to pick up some groceries while we're out, so let's make a quick stop." We pulled into the grocery store parking lot. Jack and I were a couple of guys on an important mission: lunch, groceries, and maybe a treat or two.

We got a shopping cart and made our way through the store. As we approached the checkout line, a toddler threw herself on the floor screaming. She apparently wanted the candy bar and gum her mother was returning to the shelf. Even though the mother attempted to distract her, the child was intent on the lost prizes.

Jack folded his arms across his chest, shook his head, and looked up at me.

"She's lost her humor, Poppa."

Life Lesson

As I laughed, I reflected on the wisdom in Jack's statement. How many of us throw our own version of a temper tantrum when life doesn't go as we wish? When someone grabs our parking spot or the traffic doesn't move fast enough? When our expectations are not met, do we throw our own little fit? Have we learned the value of seeing the positives in a situation—of laughing at life?

Jack's lesson was a good one: when we don't get what we want or things don't go exactly according to plan, take a deep breath and relax, smile, or laugh out loud. Life is better when we don't "lose our humor."

14

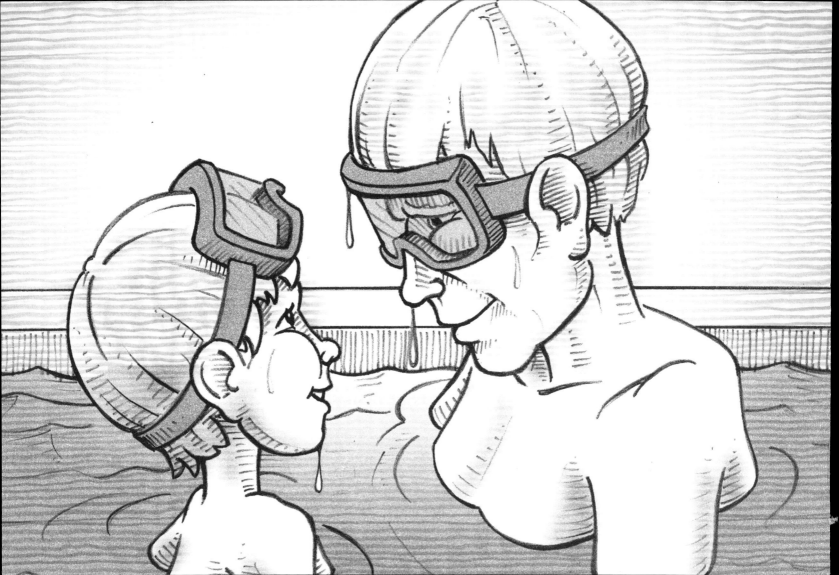

Stay in the Pool a Little Longer

Jack's high-pitched yell warned us that a cannon-ball splash was about to drench us. He got a kick out of splashing us. Three generations—Grammy and me, Jack's parents, and Jack, Ally, and Tommy—savored a refreshing dip in the pool under the hot Arizona sun. Most of all, we celebrated the chance to be together again.

Jack's family had moved from Dallas to Phoenix, and we were having "grandchildren withdrawals." Being long-distance grandparents wasn't as much fun as when they lived near us.

When everyone else abandoned the pool in search of lunch, Jack swam to me. With face mask perched on top of his head, he climbed on my knee and said, "Poppa, let's stay and play a little longer. We need more time together!"

So, even though our skin was wrinkled like prunes, we stayed. After all, only good buddies could know the value of several more jumps into the deep end and holding their breath under water for a count of twenty-five!

Life Lesson

At a very young age, Jack understood the power of persuasion. He knew the exact words to convince me to stay in the pool—"we need more time together." Jack communicated how he really felt: he missed me! And I, surely, missed him, too.

Jack's simple request reminded me to take advantage of our moments together, to be willing to invest a little more time in each other. As the familiar saying goes, no businesspeople on their deathbeds wish they had spent more time at the office. Jack's message in the pool that day continues to challenge this grandpa and grandma to take advantage of those magic moments with loved ones, to relish the opportunities to stay in the pool a little longer.

PLANET PLUTO

Jack got right to the point one evening.

"Poppa and Grammy, my mommy saw on TV that Pluto isn't a planet anymore."

"We heard the same thing, Jack. What do you think?"

"I don't think it's fair!"

"Why not?"

"Well, just because Pluto is smaller than the other planets doesn't mean it isn't one."

"You're right, Jack. It isn't fair."

"Pluto will always be my favorite planet!"

Life Lesson

Long ago, I learned to respect the contributions of modern inventions. Where would we be without the wheel, lightbulb, car, airplane, and air conditioning? Science invites us to examine our world with fresh eyes. It makes our lives easier, but sometimes we're tripped up when we become too scientific.

Jack didn't like this new science fact—the deletion of Pluto from the list of planets. Pluto will always have a special place in Jack's heart.

Our grandson has an instinctive sense of fairness and isn't afraid to voice his opinion. Even though his objections can't change the fact that Pluto is no longer considered a planet, he feels it isn't fair. His stubborn resistance causes me to chuckle—and reminds me that it's OK to cling to what you think is right.

I agree with Jack that Pluto is important. We all remember the days of listening for Santa and the reindeer on the roof on Christmas Eve. Didn't we all peek under our pillows to see what the tooth fairy left behind? The "experts" may claim that Pluto is no longer a planet, but Jack and I will stand firm as we look through our telescope in search of planet Pluto.

Just a Few Words . . .

"Juice, Poppa."

"Gammy."

"Peeeez!"

"Blankie."

The early infant and toddler days passed at rocket speed. The initial attempts at words quickly gave way to real conversations. We no longer need an interpreter to understand Jack. Good thing, too, because he has a lot to say.

"Grammy, I've got an idea."

"Great, Jack! I can't wait to hear it."

When Jack is visiting, the ideas come from all directions. Talking is the way our little guy sorts out his world. His mind revs to a higher level each time he discusses his ideas. My contribution to our conversations is often simply to listen. Paying attention to his chatter helps him grow and gives us a perspective we don't find anywhere else.

Life Lesson

The author of the old adage, "children should be seen and not heard," didn't know much about children, and certainly not about Jack. His thoughts—from a five-year-old perspective—prove to be surprisingly insightful at times. Other times, his tokens of wisdom are downright funny. At any rate, encouraging the discussion is good for all of us.

When he was just beginning to talk, at times I couldn't quite understand him, but we were both persistent and worked it out together. Once in a while, a little quiet time would have been nice, but then I would have missed a whole lot of Jack. So I often find myself saying, "Hey Jack, what's going on?"

CHOOSE YOUR WORDS WISELY

The siren announced to the world that Grammy had been caught speeding. Grammy stopped the car while Jack bombarded her with questions from his car seat.

"What's going to happen, Grammy?"

As Grammy scrambled for her driver's license and tried to compose herself before the police officer appeared at her window, she tossed Jack a quick answer.

"The policeman might give me a ticket. Grammy might go to jail."

She was kidding, of course, but those words came back to haunt Grammy. In the days that followed, whenever Grammy's name came up, sometimes at the most inopportune times, Jack informed others of his grandmother's "criminal" background.

"If that happens, boom! Grammy goes to jail!"

Life Lesson

In Grammy's desire to teach Jack the importance of following the law and obeying police officers, she hastily offered Jack an explanation for her predicament. Jack's constant parroting of her exact words showed us—and those we were around—that he understood the gravity of the situation. Jack had a clear grasp of the concept that consequences follow our actions. He certainly got the point!

Jack taught us something else, though. His continual retelling of the event and Grammy's statement about "going to jail" emphasized the importance of carefully choosing our words. We're likely to hear them again and again.

We eventually convinced Jack that Grammy was a law-abiding citizen, and he wouldn't really have to visit her in jail. Jack learned the importance of obeying the law, and we learned that young ears are always listening.

STARGAZING TOGETHER

Jack tugged on my sleeve, and I leaned down. He cupped his hand over my ear, and Grammy watched as we nodded in agreement and slipped away as our group got ready to begin the cookout. There was time for food later; we had work to do. We took off to the side of the house.

"Poppa, if you lie down with your arms under your head, you can see millions of stars. Try it!"

And that's the way Grammy found us ten minutes later, when her curiosity led her to our getaway location. Jack and I sprawled on the driveway, gazing at the stars. I was glad Jack had whispered his invitation into my ear at the picnic table:

"Poppa, do you want to look at the stars with me?" It was an invitation that was hard to turn down.

We regularly look for the Big Dipper and the Little Dipper. I'm still not sure I can make out Orion, but Jack tells me it's there. I may not be an expert on stars, but I'm certain that I'm privileged to be Jack's stargazing buddy.

Life Lesson

In moments like these, Jack reminds me to be fascinated with our world. His thrill over discovery energizes me. Jack's wonder with creation inspires me to view life with a fresh perspective and to soak up the sweetness of simple, special moments.

The bigger lesson Jack teaches me in our stargazing moments is to savor time together. Orion can remain a mystery for life, as long as Jack continues to unveil the wonder of his heart to me. Searching the night sky for twinkling lights can't compare to the treasure of knowing each other.

Stay on the Sidewalk

Jack and I walked to our favorite after-gymnastics destination for Jack's favorite treat—vanilla milk. As we hurried along the sidewalk, Jack reached for my hand.

"Poppa, hold my hand. If you fell off the sidewalk, a car could hit you and BAM! You'd be in the hospital!"

Jack had listened all those times I'd said almost the same words to him. He understood the importance of looking both ways at the intersection, holding hands in traffic, and staying on the sidewalk—good advice that he obviously believed. On this afternoon, the advice came full circle, back to me.

I chuckled at the seriousness of his warning and reached for his hand.

Life Lesson

I wondered about how many more remarks Jack has grabbed ahold of when we speak. What else can I teach him? How can I impact Jack's life beyond simple safety instructions? How can I prepare him to protect himself in other ways? How can I instruct him in guarding his mind, will, and emotions and in protecting the treasures of his heart? How can I teach him to reach out but also remember to stay on the sidewalk in some situations?

We got the vanilla milk.

"Please hold my hand! Stay on the sidewalk, Poppa!"

I grabbed Jack's hand and caught a glimpse of urgency in his eyes. I squeezed his hand a little tighter and walked carefully down the sidewalk.

THREE MAGIC WORDS

Jack splashed in the pool with his sister, Ally, and his brother, Tommy. Lunch and cartoons followed the swim. Sleepovers with grandkids are God's reminders of why we had kids early in life, in the days when we had a little more energy. Spending time with our grandkids is still the highlight of many of our days.

Grammy bathed the kids and helped them don their pajamas. As we tucked them in to bed and said our prayers, Jack made a pronouncement loud and clear.

"Grammy and Poppa, we will always love you!"

Life Lesson

Jack's simple statements about love served as a wonderful reminder to this grandpa and grandma of how special the words "I love you" really are.

In a world that teaches men to be tough and a culture that sometimes ridicules male tenderness, we're proud of our grandson. Saying those words is such a natural part of Jack's life that he proclaims them with conviction and without hesitation. Jack can teach us older guys to be unashamed in our affection for our families and to be a little quicker with our I-love-you's.

PANCAKES AND TRAINING WHEELS

Jack explored the syrup options on the table while he waited for his pancakes. It was quite a selection—maple, strawberry, all the good stuff. Breakfast together at the local pancake house was a treat our family often enjoyed on Saturday mornings. The food was good, and we used the time to update each other on the highlights of the week. Soon the food arrived, and as Jack, Ally, and Tommy buttered their steaming stacks of pancakes, a neighbor passed our table.

"Hey, neighbor. Getting ready for a big weekend?" we called out.

We fell into a conversation about local events, the PTA, and the upcoming play day at school when Jack decided it was his turn to be included. He raised his hand.

"Mrs. Cox, my dad took the training wheels off my bike today!"

We all laughed as Mrs. Cox congratulated Jack on his graduation from training wheels.

Life Lesson

Jack didn't exactly enter the conversation on the same wavelength as the adults, but he wanted to be a part of the conversation. He didn't let the adult topics keep him from jumping in. He had something important to tell everyone and felt the freedom to steer us in another direction. Hopefully, he knew we all cared about what was important to him and that we'd want to hear what he had to say.

At any rate, Jack felt secure that he was with people who loved him and wanted him to be in the conversation, too. Don't we all need a place to shout out our victories—to celebrate our milestones? Even adults long for relationships that encourage us to share our big, and small, accomplishments.

Pancakes and training wheels? Hey, they work for us!

"Please Leave a Message"

"At the sound of the beep, please leave a message, and we'll call you right back."

While we adults are accustomed to dealing with voice mail, Jack wasn't. He was greeted by our recorded message on his first chance to call us himself. Here's what we heard on our end of the phone when we pushed our playback button:

"Hello, Poppa, this is Jack calling. Hello, hello—Mommy, he's there, I heard him talk, but he's not talking now!"

"What did he say, Jack?"

"He said to leave a message."

"Okay, go ahead and leave a message."

"Message!"

Life Lesson

We laughed to hear him say "Message"! Jack had followed instructions perfectly! Good job, Jack! Voice mail was hailed as another wonderful invention years ago and has also been the subject of many jokes. Haven't we all wanted to leave a clever message when we hear the familiar, "Please leave a message, and we'll call you right back"?

Jack demonstrated how to handle his confusion—he asked for help. Then he did exactly as he was told and said, "Message," loud and clear.

"I WANTED TO GET A RUNNING START!"

Tommy and Ally hugged us, but Jack backed away several feet. *Uh-oh!* For a split second, Grammy and I looked at each other, thinking maybe Jack thought he was getting too old for good-bye hugs and kisses. So, we asked if he was going to give us a hug and kiss as he usually did. Jack looked at us as he started running toward us and matter-of-factly answered: "I wanted to get a running start!"

Another time, when Jack was leaving for a one-week camp, he displayed his usual enthusiasm for the good-bye ritual.

"Grammy, I'm going to give you two hugs and two kisses. One is for right now, and one you can save for later!"

Jack knows how to offer his affection enthusiastically to people he loves. He needed to get a running start to shower us with his love, and he wasn't stingy with the offering.

His two-for-one offer said it all. Grammy would need two hugs and kisses—he knew she would miss him. As a six-year-old, he intuitively grasped that touch points assure family and friends we love them.

Life Lesson

Jack teaches us to slow down and take the time to share a memorable moment at each parting. "See you later" and "take care" aren't enough in Jack's good-bye system. "Let's do lunch sometime" is too vague for Jack. He wants the running start. He gives the double scoop of affection; one hug simply isn't enough.

When Jack prepares to depart, he gets a running start on his hugs and doles out an extra helping of love to the lucky ones saying good-bye. How's your running start?

Jack the Critic

Four "grammies" and seven grandkids filed into the theater. The play's posters promised a captivating story. The colorful cartoon artwork said children would love it—or so Grammy thought. The lights dimmed, and the music began. Seven pairs of eyes stared at the stage, anticipating elaborate costumes, funny things to happen, and lots of action. Four other pairs of eyes watched the seven kiddos.

Unfortunately, no one checked out the reviews before caravanning to the theater. About fifteen minutes into the performance, Jack leaned over to whisper, "Grammy, this play needs to be over—now!"

Jack proved that anyone can be a critic, and kids make some of the best. They're candid and don't hold back. Much like the kid in the crowd of *The Emperor's New Clothes*, they often blurt out the obvious. When adults are too polite to speak the truth, kids will speak up: "Hey, the emperor doesn't have any clothes on!"

Life Lesson

We adults can learn from Jack. Don't be afraid to offer a critic's review, even if it isn't glowing. How much time do we waste dancing around a subject we don't really want to address? When did we become so shy about offering an honest assessment of something? Jack taught Grammy that day that sometimes we need to provide an honest perspective and to do it with a sense of urgency. It's okay to be honest, and Jack certainly was.

THE EASTER EGG HUNT

The annual Easter egg hunt was about to begin. Colorful eggs dotted the field. Pinks, yellows, and reds, and all the colors of the rainbow decorated the landscape in front of the eager boys and girls. Some kids shyly took their place at the starting point, while others lined up in sprinters' stances with buckets in hand. Parents and grandparents yelled last-minute instructions and encouragement to their little ones.

I leaned over to Jack and whispered, "All of the kids will go to the closest eggs. Can you run to the big tree? You might be first to pick up the eggs under the tree."

Jack nodded, took off, and coolly filled up his bucket under the shade of the big tree while the others battled closer to the starting line. Jack came back with a bucket full of eggs.

"Poppa, thanks for the tip!"

Life Lesson

Jack appreciated my little nugget of wisdom, and he put it into action. There's a lesson here for all of us: be willing to offer help in the form of understandable, logical advice, and, if you're the one on the receiving end, be willing to think about it and give it a try.

Jack could've been tempted to follow the herd of kids and try to get some eggs for his basket. Instead, he listened to trusted advice and delayed filling his bucket a split second longer than the other kids. In the long run, he collected some great eggs and didn't have to battle with the masses. He experienced the added benefit of enjoying the shade of the big tree during the hunt. On a warm, sunny day, that's a big bonus!

CAUGHT!

Grammy walked into the TV room where Jack, Ally, and Tommy sprawled across the floor watching their favorite cartoon. Grammy glanced at Jack and smiled.

"How was the cookie?"

Jack had a shocked look and then gave Grammy a crumb-covered grin. "How'd you know, Grammy?"

Cookies and cookie jars—appealing to almost everyone and irresistible to grandkids! Jack was caught, even though he thought he'd hidden the evidence.

Life Lesson

We all know the feeling. We were sure we could sneak through a changing yellow light or roll through that stop sign. No one was around to see. Surely, this one time wouldn't matter. Just when we think we've gotten away with something, someone finds us out.

A good lesson for Jack—don't ever think you can fool life. Making exceptions to fudge the rules or to take a shortcut usually ends with consequences that fill us with regret. Don't make a habit of deception. Learning to be honest and look people in the eye with a clear conscience is a worthy goal.

Living with a clear conscience also gives us a sense of confidence. We can face life with a smile because we have nothing to hide. Living honestly produces a freedom void of the fears of hearing an "Aha! Caught you!"

In Jack's case that day, he enjoyed a cookie. He also learned not to hide because someone would find out his secret. Jack's cookie-crumb-coated grin reminds us that it's a good thing to tell it like it is.

SOME SPECIAL FRIENDS

Grammy and the grandkids hopped out of the car for a special birthday event. This celebration included grandmothers, grandkids, and cartoon characters. Kids and grandmothers alike anticipated a fun-filled birthday party at a local restaurant, featuring waitstaff dressed as Spider-Man, Cinderella, Captain Marvel, and other children's heroes.

After a meeting, I arrived as the party was ending and chuckled at Jack's parting with his new comic-book friends.

"Bye, Spider-Man!"

"Bye, Jack."

"Bye, Superman!"

"Bye, Jack."

"Bye, Captain Marvel!"

"Bye, Jack."

Life Lesson

When did my grandson acquire first-name status (albeit aliases) with these restaurant employees? Somehow, a four-year-old had wiggled his way into the hearts of strangers in less than two hours. Jack has a way with people.

What's his secret? He's fun to be around. He isn't afraid to get close to people, ask questions, and welcome others into his world. Jack enjoys others, and, consequently, he's enjoyable to be around.

We often tell our kiddos to "have fun" as they run out the door to an event. Maybe we should include another suggestion: "be fun." Sometimes we need the reminder to focus on others instead of ourselves, something Jack seems to know naturally. Reaching out to others is part of who he is. Jack takes the time to know others and to be known—a big lesson from a little guy.

THE "CLEAN PLATE CLUB"

Dinner, vegetables, and grandparents form a combination sure to spark a plea of "Do I have to eat the peas?" from the grandkids. Grammy and I have grown adept at maneuvering around Jack's request to avoid eating vegetables.

"Just eat two more bites and then you can have dessert." The negotiations stop.

One evening, we looked at Jack's plate and discovered the veggies were gone. Jack was just putting his fork down, and we commented about the clean plate.

"We didn't know you liked carrots and peas so much, Jack."

"I don't, but they're good for my body."

Life Lesson

We worked to hide our surprise and our grins. Our Jack had grown up, at least in the vegetable-eating realm. His mom and dad's sage advice that veggies are good for your body had taken hold. Jack's matter-of-fact approach to an undesirable task not only impressed us—his attitude inspired us.

Jack demonstrated a willingness to tackle an unpleasant task head-on, get it done, and go on. He displayed a maturity that many adults don't possess. Jack understood that difficult jobs don't just go away because we wish them to disappear; he knew it took work to complete a difficult assignment.

Jack also recognized a payoff was involved—dessert! He was confident that a benefit would come as a result of his determination to stick to the mission.

Jack challenged us that day to look at hard jobs with a fresh perspective. Maybe the only motivation is that it's good for us. Maybe it will help others. Maybe it's one of those things you just have to do—paying bills or taxes, for example. Whatever the situation, the key is to take on the dreaded task, do it, and move on.

GAME ON

Bedtime usually means a bath, jammies, a book or two, and turning off the light before closing the door. Five seconds later, we hear the familiar "I'm scared!" or "I'm thirsty!" stall tactic.

The kids' mission is to prolong the evening, while Grammy and I are ready to bring the evening to a close. The game is on.

One bedtime, Jack tried a different approach.

"Poppa and Grammy, where does the light go when you turn it off?"

We had no idea how to answer his question, so, for the moment, he won the delay-the-bedtime game. Plus, we were amused at the creativity of his question, so we stayed a bit longer and attempted to answer him. Jack demonstrated a certain "brightness" in his question. He figured out that the game needed some fresh ideas to be effective, so he employed a new approach. And it worked—if only briefly.

Life Lesson

Can we all learn a lesson from Jack? When something isn't working, try something new. Don't keep using ineffective techniques. Stretch. Grow. Look at all possibilities. Have the courage to try a different approach.

We laughed at Jack's innovativeness. He stumped us for a few seconds, but only a few seconds. We took just a moment to jump back in the game. Where does the light go?

"The light goes up to the sky to help the sun get ready for a new day!" Grammy responded. "Goodnight Jack."

The door closed and the contest was over—at least for one night!

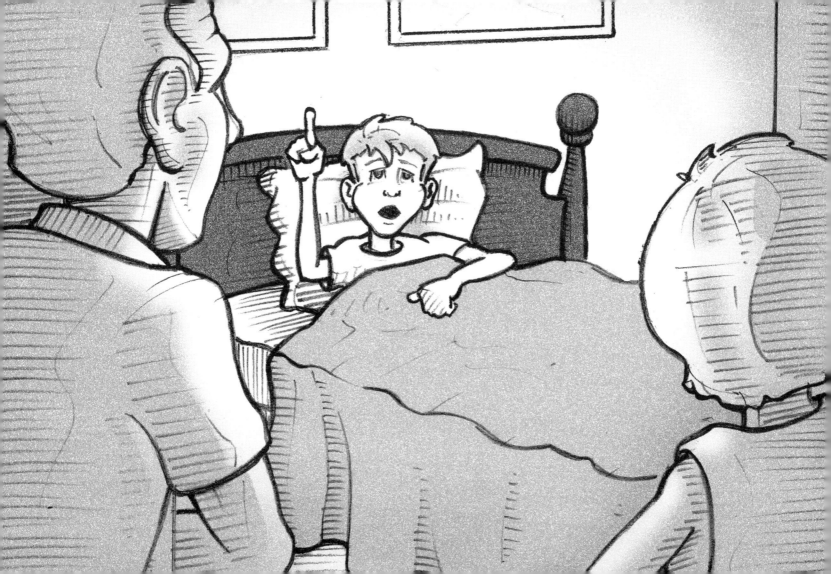

THE LIBRARY

It must be in men's DNA. There aren't any published figures, but most men like to read in the bathroom. My dad read the paper, I do the same thing, and my informal poll suggests that many other men do as well.

One day, Jack proudly announced to us that he was now able to go to the bathroom "all by myself." Clearly a breakthrough to remember. He took off for the bathroom and a couple of minutes later, a small voice asked, "Poppa, can I have something to read?"

Of course I wanted to be of help, so I looked around for something he would enjoy. I grabbed a large book from our coffee table with pictures of dogs on the cover. *He'll like this*, I said to myself confidently as I handed it over, and closed the door.

A couple of minutes later, he came out with the book in his hands.

"How did you like the book, Jack?"

"It was too heavy, Poppa! Next time, I'll take Dr. Seuss with me."

Life Lesson

I couldn't help but smile as I nodded my head and returned to my newspaper. Was it part of the "rite of passage" we had just experienced or simply one more young man joining our select reading club?

Your Words Come Bouncing Back

Jack, Tommy, and Ally often accompanied Grammy and me on errands around town. As we walked out of the grocery store one afternoon, we passed a family friend and I called out, "Hey, Tuck, how're you doing?"

A week later, Jack and I walked to a nearby park, talking along the way. At the park, we tossed a ball around for a while. Soon Jack held the ball for a moment and looked at me.

"Hey, Poppa, how's Tuck?"

Life Lesson

Jack's question startled me. He remembered my friend's nickname, and it came to his mind randomly as we played catch. I was amused that he spoke Tuck's name with familiarity. I realized how much information our grandkids hear and store away for another time. I felt challenged to make all my conversations appropriate for little minds.

How can we provide noteworthy memories for our grandkids on a day-to-day basis? Is our speech uplifting to them? Does it make them think? Have we communicated clearly to young minds? When we say something, do they hear something different? Are we giving them good ideas to store in their memory banks to retrieve later?

How do we talk about others? Do we speak about the good things we see in them, or do we too often display a critical attitude? Do we model to the next generation a positive outlook on life? We've got to remember just how much impact we have on the lives of these little people.

Jack's mention of Tuck, reminded me how much our grandkids absorb and remember. They're watching and listening, and we have a responsibility to give them something worthwhile to remember.

Acknowledgments

Every author needs "good copy," and our grandson Jack provided the raw material for this book. I was traveling a great deal during Jake's early years, so many of the things he said to us and others got written down on airline tickets or hotel receipts. Over time Sandy, my bride of over four decades, and I would look at them, and we just knew there was a story waiting to be told.

With the support of our family and the great team at Brown Books, we got the first and subsequent drafts finished. Milli Brown, Kathryn Grant, Dr. Janet Harris, Jayme Durant, Jessica Kinkel, and Jennifer Allen made the publishing process smooth as silk. Bill Young, our illustrator, did a terrific job of capturing the images we were looking for, especially young Jack.

Now we only wait for your stories about your kids and grandkids and the great things they have to say. Just email me at rah@anet-dfw.com and the sequel to *What Jack Taught Grandpa* will include the best stories we receive from you, our readers.

Top: Tommy, Sandy, and Jack. Bottom: Bobby, Bob, and Ally.

About the Authors

Bob and Sandy Heckman have decades of professional and personal experience in business and education. Bob held sales and marketing roles with companies such as IBM and Accenture while Sandy taught in public schools for more than twenty years. As proud parents of two daughters and grandparents of four grandchildren, they've been delighted to capture many priceless quotes from kids over the years. In *What Jack Taught Grandpa*, the cartoons and life lessons help bring each quote to life—showing readers that viewing life through the eyes of a child is both rewarding and fun!

Bob and Sandy are both accomplished athletes, having competed in seventy-five marathons between the two of them, including the famed Boston Marathon and the New York City Marathon. As coauthors, they plan to conduct workshops for the educational world to share the joys of being a parent, becoming a grandparent, and learning from the children around you!